Love Light And Lot More Hope

A Poetry Collection

DIVYA ANANDAN

Love Light And Lot More Hope

Dedicated to each soul of the world
who really make it a world

i'll write for the stars and sky
for my lifetime

this book is for those
whose nights are long,
keeping dreams awake,
who hears so much,
but speaks to the wind,
who drinks the pain,
but serve the kind,
who loves so much,
but hurt too much,
who lives in the dark,
but lights so marked,
who doped the hope,
just overdosed,
who smile so bright,
like the only light,
who's not just soul,
but a magic in whole,
do you know who?
it's you,
dear you, just for you!

ACKNOWLEDGMENT

I thank my dad, my guardian angel, for always being with me no matter what happens. I thank my family members and friends who have always been by my side and supported me.

I like to thank each known and unknown faces who have appreciated my art. Those are the words that always make me to write more.

I thank dear universe for always giving words, for always blessing me with words.

I thank the words for always never betraying me, always finding a way to me.

I thank all the love, light, and hope I have in my life so that I was able to write this book to my readers to transcend love, light and a lot more hope to my readers.

Finally, I thank you, my dear reader, for choosing this book.

PROLOGUE

You know people who appreciate art are lucky; to feel what someone feels like is indeed a blessing, and I thank you reader, for picking this book. You ended up here by knowing me or not knowing me, maybe a friend of me, or a colleague, or a cowriter, or an unknown person but I would like to thank you; it's you people who walk around with stories, emotions, it's you who have inspired me or someone else to create art. And we writers always write to you, for you, about you; you are the art we artists create.

Dear reader this book is not a guide to your life, but it's a little window from your room, from where you can see pictures of the world, the rushing vehicles, big trees, and carefree children running around; someone waiting for the bus a long time, someone missing the bus a few steps away; an old man selling some bubble wand; and a young girl in her 20s buying it and blowing around the bubbles and laughing; a man all alone seated in a teashop with a train of thoughts running; scenes of the whole universe, the stars, the moon, the sunset hue, the people, the love, the pain, the hope, and everything and every little thing.

I don’t want to actually disappoint you; this book is not going to save you or change your life, but all I hope is that somewhere a piece of a writeup or at least a line will give you a little warmth; maybe some line could make you smile realising someone thinks like you, or someone feels like you; some line may comfort you thinking that we all humans share pain in different ways; some line may make you feel seen; some line may make you feel heard.

I guess there will be some page in this book that you would fold the corner, or double stroke the line, or put some bookmark, some page that could be a warm hug to you whenever your heart turns cold.

And all I hope is you get all the love and all the light and much more and more hope. And you truly deserve it, beautiful soul.

she is not a queen
she is not a princess
she is she

~ her identity

you are not a mess
maybe you are
too much
to people's
knowledge

maybe they little
know you
or either don't

you lay on
the clouds
and dream
about the stars
but girl,
you own the sky

~ *your power*

i've turned to a
person
to whom
the city lights
seems to be harsh

and the starlight
seems to be soft
somewhat
peace to chaos

you were always
fascinated
with those larger
meteoroids
busy chasing the
shooting star

but you never knew
even the shooting star
silently wished
to fall for you

~just for you

to look back, you were all in the same place, and now things have changed a lot.

it's been a while since you texted your best friend, you see your old school, not so close friend story highlights of exploring cities, and your dear one got engaged, but you weren't able to make it, and now you feel so guilty

you forgot to wish on your cousin's birthday and ended up writing a sorry note,

and the fact that you can't make time not because your busy, but because it's just somewhat tiring, tiring to just be at the same place

it's kind of hard when life has just run so fast, and yet you're at the same place,

it's so hard to see the whole world just moving around and people shifting, and you have no idea where you are and what you are up to

this life is a journey, sometimes you are just stuck, just lost, but you are on the road, it's okay to be slower than others in reaching the destination, and it’s okay in not even knowing the destination

people have their own definition of success, and it's not necessary for yours to fit in with theirs; and just think what could life be? it's actually not about success; it's just living, living in your phase, and you are successful in your own phase to win or lose doesn't make sense, to live is the one; and that's beautiful; enjoy it, live it, celebrate life, and celebrate all those wins and losses

was life a journey?
if so,
whether it's mine or
someone else?

let the path may mold
or destruct me
let i get the courage
to take the new paths
the untravelled ones
getting lostfinding new
it's truly worth it
when the
journey is mine

why there is consistent
writing about healing?

because there is
constant heartbreaks
and endless craving
to get healed

being alone and
lonely differs
at times being in crowd
we may feel
lost and lonely
and being alone
we may feel
accompanied

i don't want to be
the best version
i don't want to be
a rose in
the garden
it's okay if i
am a thorn
and i know
even the dead
roses are red
i just want to be
a version of me
a version of
only me
it's damn me

and i hope
love is
beautiful someday

the right love
will feel like
love one day

there goes this music in the background, some in pairs at dance, some in groups here and there making conversation, between all these i'm there trying to hold that glass perfectly as if not to show that i'm a newbie to parties

people smiling, talking, dancing, a lot of joy, but i feel quite lost. i feel kind of not belonging to. i stepped back and walked towards the end of the room and slowly leaned on the wall holding the glass in hand, just pretending to exist in the party, i watched around the room and saw that glass in my hand that was filled till the rim, and someone laughed i just turned in the direction of the sound and found you. someone the same way leaned on that wall with a glass filled to the rim. and i saw that glass in your hand and smiled. we laughed together. i wondered what that kind of thing was; we never talked, but we understood each other

and then this not so familiar song plays in the background. i smiled and thanked the man who played it, as it was my favourite one. and i couldn't resist tapping my feet and singing along. and i could see, you were blank. i realised that you've never heard that one, but you still enjoyed it seeing the way i enjoy it

you held my hand and pulled me into the crowd and i stood still. you started to sway and slay to the beats, i just stood and watched you enjoy my favourite song. and i too wished to dance over, as it was my favourite one; even though i know i'm a bad dancer, i just felt like going ahead, just not care about anything, to embrace the moment, to live it. and i still wonder how i started to dance over, breaking all the cold walls, and how warm and comfortable you made me feel and made me be me

we started to dance in the crowd

we danced and danced and danced

and i slipped your hand in the crowd

and you vanished

to be honest, i didn't search for you like i didn't feel like searching for you, i just thought you were one among many

but now there are places i go, and everywhere i wish to meet someone like you

you were like that cold breeze on the long tiring journey, that calms and comforts, and you were someone who made me comfortable in that place.

i think it's the little things we do to make someone feel comfortable, but those little things need some effort from inside to do it.

and all i wish to say is; be that little warmth to those cold hearts. it's okay to take little efforts to break someone's cold wall and let them breath at ease.

nothing stays
everything passes
it's all just amidst
everything will
be there
still, you need to
find a reason
to smile, to heal

between the lines
behind the
metaphors
you, me
we always live

~ *art breathes endless*

maybe love
is not complicated
maybe love is easy
it's about the simple things

like you don't need to
catch the stars for her
but just share the arms
and watch it together

on that bridge
under the river flows
and above the stars shine
between those busy people
and rushing cars
you'll find someone
holding the railing so tight
and stare at the sky

you'll find someone
with whom you can
talk about the stars for hours
and under the sky
you'll write poetries
and read it to the stars
you'll meet that
someone who is meant to be
you people will be like
you were meant to be

and i write
not that
people will hear

i write because
i don't want to
leave things unsaid

maybe in life, we all are travellers, mere wanderers. from time to time, we trip destination to destination, we reach new places, we meet new people, we get inhabited to that, and then the time plays

one day you would realise that you have turned clueless about what home could be; maybe you turn homeless. you realise that you can go anywhere, but nowhere you could feel it as yours, nowhere you could feel it as you belong to there

you would have reached peaks, watched the sunset and sunrise so near, you would have traversed the seas, reached the sky, caught all the stars, danced with the clouds, and recited all those poetries you wrote to the moon; probably you would have ticked all those bucket list things and one day when you turn back and look, all your so-called bucket list things would have just blurred out, what you could just see is yourself being alone

you'll realise you kept running towards things and you went so far that you just forgot your way back. you'll realise you kept running towards things so engaged that you never even realised, that you were running away from your own self, you'll realise, that all these days you've earned everything, but nothing fits in the void within you

maybe you thought things wouldn't change, your friends would stay the same, maybe you thought even after years you could recreate things and feel the same, maybe you knew that person you loved could wait for a long, there could be so many maybes, you would have your own reasons for your run, but just remember one thing, today if you open your door and reach the balcony, you'll see the wide sky with all stars awaiting your visit, the clouds will be rehearsing for the dance with you, and the moon will be eagerly waiting to hear all your poetries…and not just today, the very next day, and the next next days

the sky will wait for you for your entire lifetime, it's your dream, your destination, you could reach any time, and you need not run or fly throughout the journey. sometimes you could even take a walk on that path, admiring the little things that make the journey beautiful; maybe that's how you'll never forget your way back.

i know dreams, destinations are high things, and success is an unbeatable vibe, but still, sometimes you need to just take a walk on that path for a while.

sitting under the
night sky
on a cozy night
hearing that on loop
song
i realize
all this soul
yearns for
is some moonlight
and poetry

~art and peace come together

i guess
infinity is a
never defined
theory
and to me
art is infinity

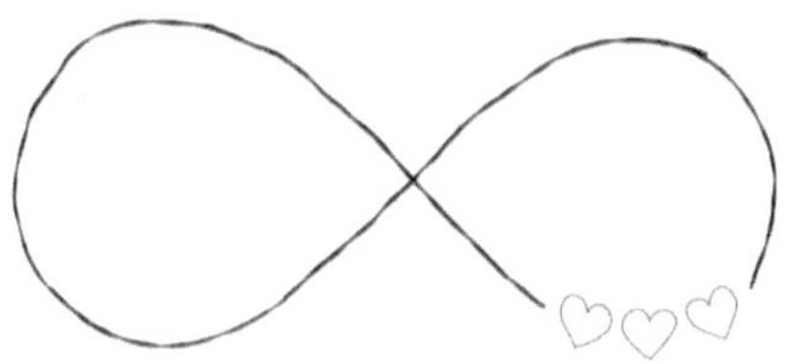

i was never
taught to love
but all i taught was
never to be
unloved
and so i love

i love
the way
you are
soft and strong

love is a mess right?
but what if the stars
don’t burn for the sky
nights won’t be that
beautiful right?

you were a kid, and all you used to do was to believe, you believed you would always get that extra piece of cake, a bigger piece of pizza

you believed you were the winner always in those board games with your family

you believed you would always be able to play cricket with your neighbourhood friend, and he would always be your teammate

you believed mom, dad, your sister, and your brother, all would always exist besides you

you believed god will always grant you whatever you asked for, those good grades, rain holidays, new cycle, and every little to bigger things

and when you were a kid all you used to do is to believe, believe and believe and now you are grown up and you understand life, that you will no longer get that extra piece of cake or a bigger piece of pizza, and now it's your turn to sacrifice it to younger ones

you understand your neighbourhood boy won't be your teammate, and you can no longer play cricket with him, he changed cities and now you barely remember his name

and all these days you weren't the real winner in board games, mom and dad always sacrificed and convinced your siblings and made you the winner

and no one stays forever; mom, dad, siblings even if they wish to keep up the promise of forever, they can't; it's just between time and existence, and we need to accept that

and you now understand god never heard and would no more grant anything, he can't change things, nor this universe, and the only hope you hold is you

to grow up; this phase you learn, unlearn, and live, and to be young is too dark, but just remember it's just a phase, it will pass by, and then if you ask me if life is going to be super cool, or all good, or sorted out after you're grown; i'll say maybe not, but now you've learned what life is, you accept things, things once that broke your heart would mend it now; things that used to hurt a lot, hurt you less

growing up is hard; to understand things is hard, to accept things is too hard, but once you learn to do that, things could be a little fine. you may feel lost, stuck, left behind, alone, broken, and nowhere feels like home, but don't worry, you'll find your way, things are all to be good.

and this heart
break heal and beat
see how strong it is
yet we have always
thought less about it

and tonight
let’s talk about
the stars
because they’ve been
hearing a hell
lot of stories

and some people
love the night sky
rooftop
caressing breeze
empty streets
long walk

and it's not that
they are neither dreamy
nor dramatic
it's that they just
find peace in them

~at least in them

never think
she was weak
as she has that
broken heart and
she loved too much

she was so strong
and brave enough
to love that much

fixing each broken piece
in the line
you'll find those remnant
broken pieces of mine

i don't know what could
fix the broken means
but i guess
to me it's poetries

~ *so sure that art heals*

you know more than the fear of being alone, we have the fear of not to be seen alone. we push ourselves to fit in at many places because we didn't want to be a sad story to anyone

and now i'm seated in a cafe at a table near the window, all alone. it's been a long time since i started visiting this café, mustering all my courage, as it's always hard to socially be in solitude. it takes a lot of courage to be alone in a crowd

and luckily, every time i check- in, this table seems to be empty. this spot and me- maybe we were destined to meet. maybe they miss me on days i don't check-in, like the way i miss them on those days. maybe; i just guess. yeah, it's just a place, but it connects differently to me i've always been on this table. the half- sipped coffee. the journal sheets fleeting in the air. i keep tapping the pen on the table. staring at the window, the big tree, the busy road. searching for words. or maybe answers. or maybe some poetry

and no matter how comfort this place gives me. there have always been people who look at me as a sad story or pity me, or they run stories in their mind of me sitting lonely

and one day i found this one person seated at my nearby table. very randomly, my eye struck that person. and i paused seeing them smiling at me. you know, mom always tells this from being a child to now - stay away from strangers. but i didn't know i couldn't resist smiling back i know it's a strange thing to do to a stranger. maybe i smiled because, to someone i wasn't a sad story. maybe someone didn't pity me. maybe i don't know why exactly

and that person didn't wait in the doorway or either i didn't wait in the doorway. we had no conversations made. and i now barely remember that person's face. even if we run into each other at some random place we may not be able to recognise each other

but something made sense to me that day. i don't know how this theory of loneliness works. because sometimes we want to be lost in the desperate need of someone to find us

sometimes we sit alone and expect someone to make their way to us and sit beside us and just ask - how you're doing. or even just sit beside. not even words are needed. just being by our side a whole crowd could make someone feel lonely. but a person, one single person, can make them feel alright. i hope someday i get the courage to smile at some lonely stranger. even though knowing it's a strange thing to do to a stranger. but yeah, it comforts them, i guess. like it did to me. and yeah, we are not a sad story; like never. sometimes we quite need to take time to change our storyline.

when you carry
peace in you
you can even
walk in a storm
with grace

and at times
all i have
and none i have
is words

maybe certain things
can only be felt
and never explained

maybe earth is
beautiful
but still the moon
feels like home

for all the rain
hail and storm
you've seen
your sky will wear
the rainbow one day

in the process
of surviving
don’t forget
the art of living

you sometimes feel like why people are constantly talking about being broken, healing, dark, light, pain. you think we make too much, we feel too much

maybe; but then what is life like?

a fairytale; that's just a fictional thing

or a happily ever after; nothing stays constant, and happiness too

or a happy ending, if only we are so lucky

life is not any of this right? from the big books, the movies with craze, to the small poetry that i write sitting in my little corner, everything has the darkest shade. one of the characters has that chronic ailment, or meets an accident, and they end up not being together. and i know that's dark, honestly, yes!

but we people can't leave the darkness, because we write truth, and the truth is darker. maybe that's why it's hard to accept, i guess. we people write about the darkest of darkest, and they are not just a poet's muse, but they are all the truth of truth

and to the world that ignores and just passes by pain, we artists who acknowledge and feel pain, may seem to be the saddest souls on this earth

and yes, definitely we too want to write about holding hands, and not about broken things, and we try to hold it in, but the tighter we hold, it gets way too easier for it to slip maybe, we people speak so much about pain, as we are a little cursed to feel things too much but never consider us weak, we speak about pain, only because we know how to turn pain into power.

and to end, cheers for every pain that made it to poetries and stories.

we all are that
little broken
and we all want to be
a little loved

i don’t
poetize pain
i just emphasize
healing

you deserve the
softness love holds
you deserve the flowers
and not just the thorns
you deserve the stars
and not just the scars
you deserve a poem
and not just being a poet

you need to be
lost between those
million stars
to find the sky
as home

even in
a million pieces
you are
home to you

you know love is complicated, but we humans, we play tough, really tough.

we all have stories, you me, the stars, the moon, the sky everything

ever seen a pair of stars in a clear sky? have you wondered when all the stars have left, why do they stay stubborn in the sky

do they love each other, or either one star loves the other star so much, but the opposite just didn't care or either the one star loves the other so much but never said, and the other one wasn't that clever to know that, or they are here sharing their moments of happily ever after

what would their story be, we don't know, you don't know my story, yes of course i don't know yours, but we all have a story, lost stories, broken stories, we all hold one so tight to heart,

sometimes we fear in love, we never let ourselves to write that story, we just wonder "would that person be that one, would that person love me back, would i leave it unsaid, would this heart carry that weigh for a lifetime"

yes of course, love is going to break us at a point, but we'll heal, it leaves a scar, that carries some memories, we'll remember them as stories, because we all need stories to scribble in our journals, we all need stories to replay in mind with the tracks in our playlist, we all need stories to keep us awake at some random night, letting us feel pain, feel love, and feel human.

and those
breaks are like
metaphor
to your heart
and i
read you
like poetry
and you are art

the way the
stars burn
for the sky
isn't love
a little
pain!

~love comes with pain

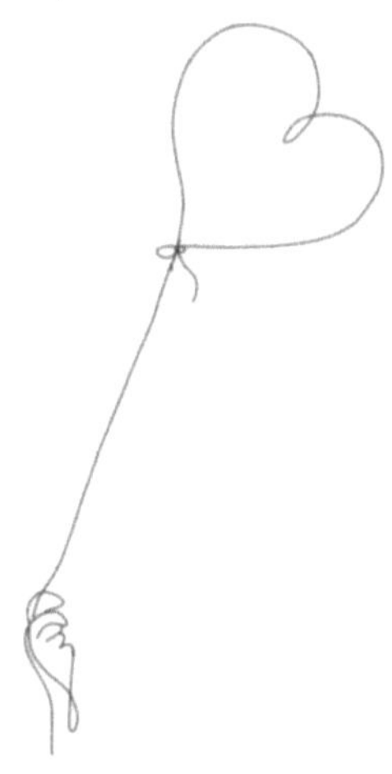

people who
love stars
are different
from people
who loves sunsets
it's a bit different
to feel comfort
in the dark
it's a bit different
to see hope
even with
a little light

the stars never
gave up
on the
darkest night

~ *little reminder*

i know you've gone
through so much
i know you are
going through so much
and i know you may
go through things yet more
but all i see is
how strong you've been
how strong you are
and how strong you are to be

i know there are many reasons for you to
never say the way you felt

i know you had more reasons to leave things
unsaid rather than the reasons to be said

it's hard to keep things in the friend zone
when you are just zoned off. to save the
bond you broke your heart

and i know it's worse when no one break
your heart, but you break it by yourself. no
one, just by yourself: i know that's worse
to this love, you don't write poetries,
because you don't want to recollect and
regret it. you leave it as an unread book on
your old shelf, that you never read but never
forget to dust it every now and then

these words from me aren't to just dust out those memories, or to say you were right or wrong, whatever it may be, you said or never said to that one person you loved, you stood with courage between love and friendship, nothing could be said as right or wrong in love

and yes, to save the bond, you even broke your own heart, you were never timid, you said or never said, you had the courage to do any of it, both needs courage, and yes love needs courage, you had it
and love will find its way back to you
and that's for sure!

honestly,
people don’t care about
someone hating them
but when you love them
it means so much to them
it’s so much
i guess you know
what that’s like

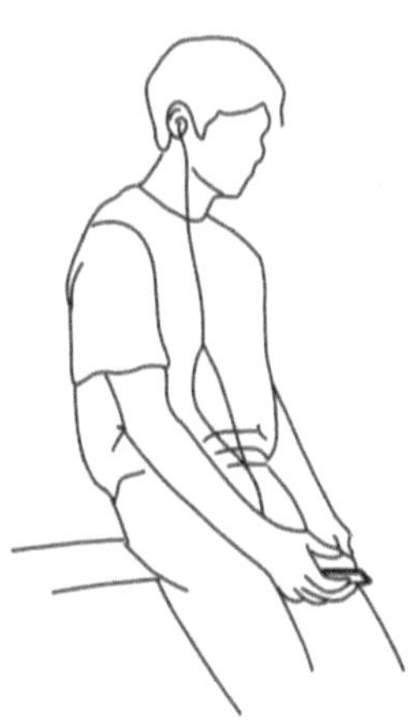

you've been admiring
the stars for a long time
but hell
i've seen a
whole galaxy in you
you are just
way more than you think

even pain could be
written in its
most beautiful way
and that's the beauty
of pain and poetry

you say she’s this much
you say she’s that much
but just explore her
you’ll see the cosmos
exploded in her
and yes she’s so much

i don't know, whether i stop
watching you on busy nights
and i start searching for you
on the loneliest nights
on every lonely night
when i search for you
you be there for me
you shine bright
maybe you tell something to me
maybe you missed me all these days
i don't know
but thank you for being there
shining bright
on every lonely night
and the stars seem to be bright
on every loneliest night

and love is that, it's like watching a melodramatic play, under dim light, and soft music, in an empty auditorium all alone. no shoulders to fix the head, no hands to wipe off tears, or no arms to embrace. yes, that's about love, something dreamy yet painful

in love, we take sufferings alone. it's not that the other person is not ready to share. they may or may not, but we love them so much that we never let them suffer

we are even ready to walk away, ready to let go of them, if that's to give them happiness. we are very deliberate to lose them, if that's the way they'd find happiness. what matters to us is just their happiness but i get you, you think how can we easily let go of someone we love and isn't love about fighting hard? but i guess love is not something to fight, to win. and maybe sometimes in love, you should lose, and that's winning

to let go isn't that we don't love them anymore. maybe to let go is to love more. maybe to love far exceedingly, that we are ready to choose pain over their happiness

because sometimes we love someone so much. much more than our own self, because we can't teach the heart to fall in measures right, it just happens

but i guess when you love someone so much, you should also learn to let go of them too because it hurts to let go, yes, it's a pain, but when you never learn to let go, and when you people are to fall apart, believe me, that apparently kills

you know this doesn't hurt
that we don't talk anymore
but this does hurt
that we talk but not
like the way we used to

~it's strange that we turned into strangers

just forgotten
how does home
feels like

~ little lost

art keeps us busy
that's why we
connect with art
that one song, that one movie
that one book, that one line
that one thing that
makes you feel better
it doesn't change things
the chaos still runs
but it's now like a soft melody
just trying to rush in your ears
while art keeps you busy

you complain her
as being hard
but her heart holds
a garden of sunflowers
and a flutter of butterflies in her
she is lovable
but you never knew
the way to love her

your stitched scars
are patchwork in heart
your broken heart
is always an art

why is it that i always lock myself on the couch; under the blanket on those rainy days and sit in the balcony and wait for the sky to rain on other days?

why does that starless sky and the moonless night depress me?

why is that always the absence that emphasizes the presence?

i had all these questions in my mind and then i realized

people are important, time is precious, and love is infinite

missing someone after you actually miss them doesn't help in any way

always remember there is no - " too long time
to love someone"

every day, every hour, every minute, every
second is precious

and love is something that doesn't bound.
how much ever love you give to people
it always feels like too little

because, all we humans need is; love, love,
and love.

it's about
the mess we write
it's about
the magic you seek

~ *poetry*

people, books, movies
they say different
things about love
different ideas of love
but everything seems
to be weird, absurd, distant
until we live that moment

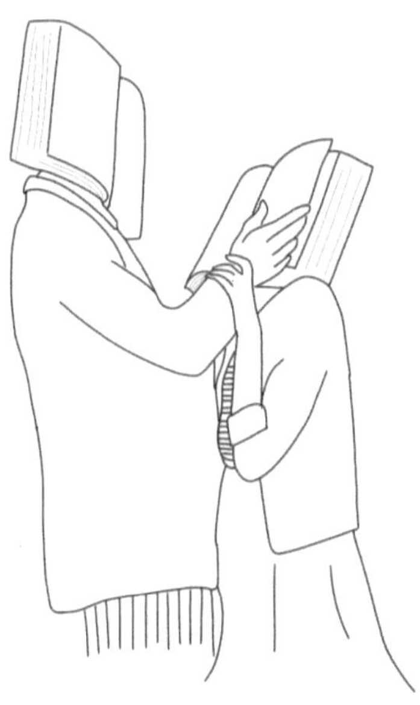

you are home
bounded
with bones

~ the peace rest in you

even when your
heart is burnt
you painted red
just loved too much
just didn’t know
how much is
too much to love

~and that's okay

and all your
bruises will
bloom
sooner or
later
but for sure

and one day in the journey of life,

the person you've been holding on too tight would say that we can't be that anymore, neither as lovers nor as those old friends, and in the journey, you'll be just left abandoned

people don't just move away, sometimes they cease the light, sometimes they cease the path, you can't just easily move on, it's really hard

and one day you both would cross paths in that familiar street, but both turn to unfamiliar faces, you'll realize that the other person has moved on happily

but you sadly will still be trying on that move on, they'll walk happy with somebody,

and you'll stand there alone and still smile seeing them being happy and even after years, you will still be experimenting on that move on, i don't say you would be trapped under those old tale sheets

you may push yourself harder and move on, but i'm sure you can't be completely off, because people change, love changes, life changes, but i guess you can't change the way your heart felt for someone right?

it's a beauty
how the sky waits
for the moon
and how the nights
turns to poetry

~ solitude

even the
fireflies and
butterflies
follows her

~ *her magic*

a number of atoms
put together made
you as a human
and this soul
is the most colourful one
it has every shade

and this world tries to
pick one and paint it

and say it's you
just see
how foolish they are

and we all
are a piece of poem
lost in the world of art
in search of words
just forgotten
we ourselves
are an art.

~you are art

if your intension
is aren’t to
give her wings
then don’t
promise her
the heaven

on a winter night, heavy rain outside, lying on the couch, you stare at the window, watching the raindrops getting shattered, a train of thoughts take a run. getting lost in thoughts, you try to fall asleep but the cold breeze hits your bare skin keeps you awake. you twist and turn on the couch but every minute leave to unslept

you always felt like not to open that old diary, with those stories of smiles, laughter, pain and cries. that diary with unsent odes and blurred photos tucked between sheets
you fear to revisit some paths. your fear is that you would be lost in that path. and you've been there, you know how hard it was to exit that road. but tonight, you take that diary in hand, you decide to take that road mustering all courage

but now you walk on that road, inhaling the air scented with memories. you run things in your mind. you remember the moments you had to tell the way you felt.

you remember the things that holded you back from telling it. you remember the moment you saw them with someone. you remember the moment you just walked away collecting all those shattered pieces

you recollect everything, but this time it doesn't hurt. the pain of not being chosen, not loved back, nothing hurts. instead, this time you see how beautiful this path looks with all the love you gave to that person

you'll realize it's not necessary to be loved back, there's a beauty in just giving, giving, and not expecting back and all you want this time is to be the sky, sun, wind, and rain on this road. just bless it with all the love you have, with all the love you can and just be the metaphor of eternal love.

and at
end
we all are
atoms
and just
belong to dust

half read books
unopened texts
long lost friends
cancelled trips
in search of a lot
in people
yet stop meeting people
a kind of thing
to be in and out
a kind of a messy soul

her hope is
that balcony
night sky
and stars

~ her hope the universe

even when you
were cursed to
dwell on earth
you blessed the earth
with your presence
oh you deserve the heaven!

breaking
yourself
and loving
someone
doesn’t
complete you

no barricade

you smile. you cry

you love each other. you hurt each other

there may be times you holded on

there may be times you walked away

and whatever you people do, this or that, you end up knowing this will never happen with anyone; and no one can make you feel this, this lot

kind of no matter wherever you go, the destination is the same; the destination is that one person

whatever you people do, love or hurt, or;
grieve or laugh; you share it

you make love

you define your love

and this world can never get that.

all i want is
more and more poetry
more and more books
more and more songs
more and more movies
more and more art
more and more empathy
more and more emotion
more and more life

~art is life

kind hearts
are never
weak
kindness
is braveness

why do you write about
the stars, the moon, the sky
i really wonder why?

because they never betray
because they never break promises
every night the stars
visit me on the lonely balcony
being the companion
in a forlorn oblivion
and this waned lady
even when she's broken
she never forgets to light me
and the sky it just follows me
wherever i go without deny
now just tell me
how could i live without
writing for them the stars,
the moon, the sky
just tell me how can i?

the orange hues of sunset
tinge the hope in my eyes,
hope that the sun has on the moon,
even the universe revolves
under the theory of hope?
then why not us?

i just don't want to make out life
just want to go with it
the flow, it's direction
it's destination
it's high
it's low
it's fall

i don't neither wish that
it had been better, nor it to be better

i just wish to be fine
fine for the place i am
just happy for who i am
and where i am

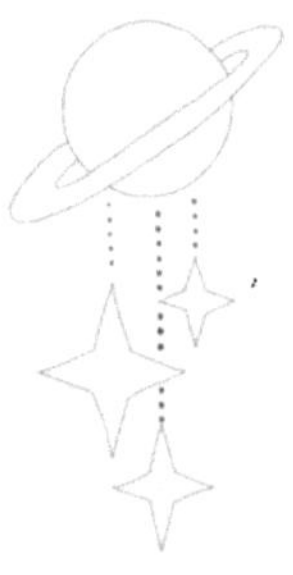

one day i ride in a metro and find someone reading my—that favourite book. you know, it first seemed normal—a metro and a book, just a normal stuff

i just plug in my earphones and scroll down the playlist. but i can't stop myself from stealing a glance every now and then to see all those little expressions that creep in when they are reading my favourite book

i see them smiling when reading, and probably guess the stuff that made them smile

i see them folding the corner of the page. it stirred something in me. i guess you know how it feels to see someone do those old-school things that we used to think we were the only one to do so my heart started to beat a little faster. and all i want now is to sit beside them and tell them all about that book

the line that i felt was just written to me
the line that gave me the coldness
the line that gave me the warmth
the line that i underlined, double stroked

you know that there are n number of songs and n number of books and n number of movies, but i wonder how i met that one favourite song on the radio in a cab ride on a busy morning to the office

i wonder how i met that book that wrecked my heart, which was lying in the corner of the bookstore with no one around, when all were grouped around some probable bestseller i wonder how i met the art of van gogh from some extreme corner of the world when all around knew da vinci for mona lisa, when all around was looking at her eyes, and all i do is stare at this man's shades of sadness

i still wonder how i ended up in that movie that makes the heart heavier and the soul lighter, on a random sleepless night, scrolling down the screens and finally felt like watching, and it ended me with tears drenched pillow

there may be even the best song, even a million-copy selling book, or the most colourful artist, or an award-winning movie, but i wonder how i met that particular art; i wonder how i met it and how it mended my life you know the type of art one person likes: the stories, poetry, and songs, it just shows how heavy their souls are, for all these art works has made them breathe and live, and has saved them. and i sometimes think art is a drug that i'm just not enough of

all these thoughts run through my mind, and i am just lost for a while. i pulled myself back and see the seat; it was empty, and i smiled thinking that i missed the person, but they have found the best art.

some of them
neither connect
with people
nor worry about
loosing people
and we always
thought that
they don't care
about people

maybe that's not right
maybe they have
loved too much
and lost so much
and now they don't think
much about loving or loosing

she is kind
of different
she travels
paris alone

~she is a magic

we grow up
we turn mature
we understand things better
we face those reality checks
and all this young age
we've heard people
praising the truth
and now the fact is that
the truth hurts the most

~to grow up is little darker

i wonder how you give so much love, even after you know, the only effort that person could take is to break your heart

even after you knew loving them would turn you broken, you still gave the heart infinite times

each time you give, each time they break

and nowadays, man you heal faster, you fix your broken heart perfectly, and you have mastered in fixing those broken pieces

people complain about you, they say you give too much

but only you know how much it takes to give that much... only you…

you are the one who has realized it's better to be unloved rather than those half love, you know the pain of half love, and so you have always given the love that person deserves and most time you gave more than they deserved

and at the end i can't even assure you, that you'll get back all the love that you have given, because you have given so much, i don't know if someone could justify, what could love be, to a heart that knows to only love.

strong, brave
bold, timid
weak, calm
chaotic
quiet, loud
these all are labels
they'd never define you

~you are more than their labels

some souls have just
stopped living for people
and just living for art
and if you ask me
oh does art heal?
i'll say
art gives life

i dream of a life
filled with
light and warmth
moonlight and sunshine
a call from the stars
for a dance in the sky

you portray her as an angel
you give her wings
but instruct never to fly
you give her a crown
but instruct never to chin up
you drape her with a gown
but intent to rip it down
she never wanted
to be an angel
all she wants is to be
a mere human being
like me, you
just a mere human being

to wear
the heart
on sleeve
you need
the right
shoulder

we walked away from each other and now meet each other in a strange city, and all these days walking around with a little hope of meeting each other, clinging at some corner of our heart

we greet each other and i ask u “are you happy’’ you pause a little and say... "yes", you ask me back i too pause a little and say... "yes" and we both knew that it was an incomplete yes

we walk down the street and you pick that favourite flowers of mine from the shop, you grasp my hand before we cross the street, you hold back the cafe door for me to enter, we order each other’s favourite on menu card and smile at each other thinking things haven't changed and yes, i don't know whether this night is a right one or a wrong one or it was a end or a beginning to something, i don't know but it just felt as a good one, somewhat comforting and this strange city felt like home tonight

i wonder why some people make us feel the same way we felt for them the very first time, to pass by years and meet people and none make you feel the same every time, but this person feels same, like those rain drop smell and the old book scents the same every time

and the night passes by, we talk over, end with a goodbye, walk away, turning around shoulder and smiling back and waving hands for every few steps we take, and we didn't change numbers, or emails, maybe we hoped to meet around each other again someday you know people say you don't choose love and love chooses you, they say love finds you, like today, on this random street of this city.

dear a once wounded heart
never lets another wound
it just protects the heart
from falling over again
and to be wounded
yet another time

i know you say your
heart is forbidden
but dear
even the bare land
blooms in right hand

~the right love

in search of words
to transcribe the unfelt
to transcribe the unexpressed
to transcribe the unlived
to transcribe the nonexistence
in search of words in reality
to express things in mirage
is what to write meant

to hold on
or to let go
the difficult was
to let go

to hold on was
to keep things
close to heart

to let go was
to let things
close to heart
to fall apart

and the love
i hold for you
is so much
and so much
and so much
that i can't
hold too much
and so i let it go
and i understand that
sometimes to love
is to let go

to be without
knowing everything
is a blessing
but we humans
aren't so lucky
unfortunately we
tend to grow up
and you know
now as a grownup
this soul so badly wants
to unlearn things
to be that child again
running across the
streets again

we were once kids and all we wanted was to grow up fast. and now all we want is to desperately be that child again and never want to grow up

yes, growing up is tricky, quite hard. you experience so much. you are meant to feel things

first time you feel what's love, what's to be loved, what's to be unloved, what's a heartbreak is

first time feeling what a soulmate kind is like, and also realizing they are all just a kind of theory

first time learning the art of making a playlist and excelling in never getting tired of hearing a song on loop first time you watch the sunset with someone you love, and also learn to watch the night sky all alone

first time to stay away from home, a kid who never felt alone, now you take a walk on that empty street, drive a long way to the beach to watch waves, to find a companion called loneliness. and you'd be thankful at least it exists

yes, definitely there are going to be too many to feel. it's going to be painful actually

and if you ask me if there is any way not to be hurt, maybe if you ignore things, you may not be hurt

but i would say feel things, feel everything, feel every little thing. don't be numb, don't have that void. it's better to have a rack full of unread books rather than an empty shelf

because maybe someday when you come across and pick a book and take a random page and you'd read a line. you'd feel like that was just written to you. just speak to you

so one day when you turn back and look, everything you've felt, everything you've holded will be worth it. they would tell you so much about life.

i just don't want
to be strong
just tired of fighting
want to just loose
those shoulders
lie back
and just take
a deep breath

~and it's completely okay

love is about
bad cries
wide smile
half-eaten plate
broken porcelain
holded hands and
feet dipped in waves
long hugs
and longing days

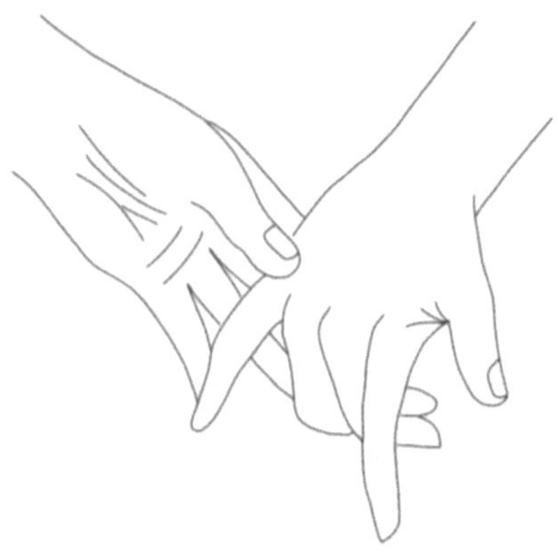

i wonder about the love
the stars and sky hold
millions of stars
this sky holds
oh, the weight it carries!
but what if this sky doesn't
love the stars anymore?
does the starless sky
still look beautiful,
or the sky doesn't
miss the stars?

what life kills
art makes it live
maybe that's why
human and art are
too much connected
art lets you breathe
and let you live

and all artist
are lost soul
giving life to souls

to hold back from groups, to be loud in silent groups

to be serious in conversations, or being in but still wandering about stars and sky, or any,

to keep speaking things or keep writing it in heart

to be different, to be weird

to be boring, to be interesting, to be beyond judgment

to never care who cares, to sing on empty roads, to dance on the terrace top

falling for unfamiliar songs, loving those unnoticeable things

whatever, whoever you may be

i just want to say to you, be you

i know it takes all courage to be you, to differ, but prefer to differ people always comment and complain on who you are

because they can never be you.

Thank you for reaching here

And completing the book

www.ingramcontent.com/pod-product-compliance
Lightning Source LLC
LaVergne TN
LVHW041100150826
845673LV00007B/1850

9798897241903